INTRODUCTION

Grand Teton National Park protects stunning mountain scenery and a diverse array of wildlife. Rising more than 7,000 feet above the valley of Jackson Hole, the Teton Range dominates the park's skyline. The elevation of the park ranges from 6,320 feet on the valley floor to 13,770 feet on the windswept granite summit of the Grand Teton.

The diverse landscapes of our National Parks system were set aside because of their incredible beauty and open spaces, making them accessible to everyone. These lands are also fragile. This requires a responsibility by visitors to experience the parks in the same spirit in which they were created: a spirit of care, appreciation and consideration for the next generation. Grand Teton National Park needs your help!

- The animals in the Tetons are wild! Help keep them alive and well. DO NOT feed any wildlife. DO NOT approach wildlife.
- While viewing wildlife, stay at least 100 yards away.
- Slow down on park roads to prevent wildlife fatalities.
- Please don't pick the wildflowers.
- Stay on trails.
- Park your vehicle only in designated areas.
- Sparkling mountain streams of the Tetons look inviting to drink, but many of them contain disease-causing bacteria. Carry plenty of fresh water while hiking.
- Enjoy, preserve and protect!

Most illustrations show the adult male in breeding coloration. Colors and markings may be duller or absent during different seasons. The measurements denote the average maximum length of most animals from nose/bill to tail tip and average height of plants. Butterfly measurements refer to wingspan. Illustrations are not to scale.

Waterford Press publishes reference guides that introduce readers to nature observation, outdoor recreation and survival skills. Product information is featured on the website: www.waterfordpress.com

Text & illustrations © 2012, 2023 Waterford Press Inc. All rights reserved. Photos © iStock Photo, Sutterstock. To order or for information on custom published products please call 800-434-2555 or email orderdesk@waterfordpress.com. For permissions or to share comments email editor@waterfordpress.com.

ISBN 978-1-58355-764-8

$7.95 U.S.

Made in the USA

GRAND TETON NATIONAL PARK WILDLIFE

A Folding Pocket Guide to Familiar Animals & Plants

GRAND TETON NATIONAL PARK WILDLIFE – A Folding Pocket Guide to Familiar Animals & Plants

WATERFORD PRESS

TREES & SHRUBS

Lodgepole Pine
Pinus contorta To 80 ft. (24 m)
Needles are twisted in bundles of 2. Cone scales have a single prickle near their outer edge.

Douglas-Fir
Pseudotsuga menziesii
To 200 ft. (61 m)
Flat needles grow in a spiral around branchlets. Cones have 3-pointed bracts protruding between the scales.

Whitebark Pine
Pinus albicaulis To 50 ft. (15 m)
Stout needles grow in bundles of 5. Egg-shaped cone has thick scales with sturdy tips.

Trembling Aspen
Populus tremuloides To 70 ft. (21 m)
Long-stemmed leaves rustle in the slightest breeze. The most widely distributed tree in North America.

Narrowleaf Cottonwood
Populus angustifolia To 50 ft. (15 m)
Slender tree grows in wet areas. Distinguished by its narrow, lance-shaped leaves.

Big Sagebrush
Artemisia tridentata To 20 ft. (6 m)
Gray-green shrub has 3-toothed, wedge-shaped leaves. Bark is gray and shredding. Plant has odor of sage.

Western Mountain-ash
Sorbus scopulina To 20 ft. (6 m)
Flowers bloom in rounded clusters and are succeeded by clusters of red berries. Common in mountain canyons.

Whiplash Willow
Salix lasiandra To 50 ft. (15 m)
Narrow leaves are green above, grayish below.

Huckleberry
Vaccinium membranaceum
To 4 ft. (1.2 m)
Bell-shaped flowers are succeeded by pea-sized, black-purplish berries in summer. Leaves turn red or purple in autumn.

Antelope Bitterbrush
Purshia tridentata
To 15 ft. (4.5 m)

Snowberry
Symphoricarpos oreophilus
To 6 ft. (1.8 m)

Chokecherry
Prunus virginiana melanocarpa
To 25 ft. (7.6 m)

Bracken Fern
Pteridium aquilinum
To 5 ft. (1.5 m)
Fronds are divided into triangular leaflets. Grows in large colonies.

WILDFLOWERS

Many-flowered Phlox
Phlox multiflora
Mat-forming plant.

Cow Parsnip
Heracleum lanatum
To 9 ft. (2.7 m)
Grows in moist soils. Creamy white flowers bloom in dense, flattened clusters.

Yarrow
Achillea millefolium
To 3 ft. (90 cm)
Leaves are fern-like.

Shrubby Cinquefoil
Dasiphora fruticosa
To 3 ft. (90 cm)
Small shrub has bright yellow, waxy flowers.

Spatterdock
Nuphar advena
To 12 in. (30 cm)
Floating aquatic plant has large leaves.

Rabbitbrush
Ericameria nauseosa
To 7 ft. (2.1 m)
Wiry shrub has erect stems that support terminal clusters of small yellow flowers.

Mules Ears
Wyethia amplexicaulis
To 32 in. (80 cm)

Goldenrod
Solidago missouriensis
To 5 ft. (2.4 m)
Yellow flowers bloom in slender, nodding spikes.

False Dandelion
Agoseris glauca
To 28 in. (70 cm)

Monkeyflower
Mimulus guttatus
To 3 ft. (90 cm)
Flowers are trumpet-shaped.

Arrowleaf Balsam Root
Balsamorhiza sagittata
To 31 in. (78 cm)
Large leaves are arrow-shaped.

Yellow Columbine
Aquilegia flavescens
To 3 ft. (90 cm)

WILDFLOWERS

Skyrocket Gilia
Gilia aggregata
To 40 in. (1 m)

Indian Paintbrush
Castilleja miniata
To 3 ft. (90 cm)

Fireweed
Chamerion angustifolium
To 10 ft. (3 m)
Common in open woodlands and waste areas.

Steer's Head
Dicentra uniflora
To 4 in. (10 cm)

Canada Thistle
Cirsium arvense
To 5 ft. (1.5 m)

Fairy Slipper
Calypso bulbosa
To 8 in. (20 cm)
Found in damp woods.

Sticky Geranium
Geranium viscosissimum
To 3 ft. (90 cm)
Leaf stems and flower stalks are sticky to the touch.

Shooting Star
Dodecatheon conjugens
To 2 ft. (60 cm)

Blue Columbine
Aquilegia coerulea
To 3 ft. (90 cm)
Blue and white flowers have long spurs.

Harebell
Campanula rotundifolia
To 40 in. (1 m)

Silvery Lupine
Lupinus argenteus
To 2 ft. (60 cm)
Note star-shaped leaves.

BUTTERFLIES

Mourning Cloak
Nymphalis antiopa
To 3.5 in. (9 cm)

American Copper
Lycaena phlaeas
To 1.25 in. (3.2 cm)

Western Tiger Swallowtail
Papilio rutulus
To 4 in. (10 cm)

Monarch
Danaus plexippus
To 4 in. (10 cm)

Western White
Pontia occidentalis
To 1.5 in. (4 cm)

Lupine Blue
Icaricia lupini
To 1 in. (3 cm)

Weidemeyer's Admiral
Limenitis weidemeyerii
To 3.5 in. (9 cm)

Pale Tiger Swallowtail
Pterourus eurymedon
To 4 in. (10 cm)

FISHES

Snake River Cutthroat Trout
Oncorhynchus clarkii behnkei
To 20 in. (50 cm)

Rainbow Trout
Oncorhynchus mykiss To 44 in. (1.1 m)

Eastern Brook Trout
Salvelinus fontinalis To 28 in. (70 cm)

Lake Trout
Salvelinus namaycush To 4 ft. (1.2 m)
Dark fish is covered in light spots. Tail is deeply forked.

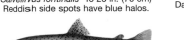

Brown Trout
Salmo trutta To 40 in. (1 m)
Has red and black spots on its body.

Arctic Grayling
Thymallus arcticus To 30 in. (75 cm)
Large dorsal fin is distinctive.

Mountain Whitefish
Prosopium williamsoni To 22 in. (55 cm)
Common in alpine lakes and streams.

Utah Sucker
Catostomus ardens To 26 in. (65 cm)

BIRDS

Great Blue Heron
Ardea herodias
To 4.5 ft. (1.4 m)

Sandhill Crane
Antigone canadensis
To 4 ft. (1.2 m)

Trumpeter Swan
Cygnus buccinator
To 6 ft. (1.8 m)
Note stout black bill.

California Gull
Larus californicus
To 23 in. (58 cm)
Note black and red spots on its bill.

Canada Goose
Branta canadensis
To 45 in. (1.14 m)

White Pelican
Pelecanus erythrorhynchos
To 5 ft. (1.5 m)

Mallard
Anas platyrhynchos To 28 in. (70 cm)

Marten

Green-winged Teal
Anas crecca To 15 in. (38 cm)

Lesser Scaup
Aythya affinis To 18 in. (45 cm)
Note peaked crown.

Common Merganser
Mergus merganser To 27 in. (68 cm)
Note slender profile and thin red bill.

Barrow's Goldeneye
Bucephala islandica To 20 in. (50 cm)
Male has a white facial crescent.

American Coot
Fulica americana
To 16 in. (40 cm)

BIRDS

Golden Eagle
Aquila chrysaetos
To 40 in. (1 m)

Red-tailed Hawk
Buteo jamaicensis
To 25 in. (63 cm)

Swainson's Hawk
Buteo swainsoni
To 22 in. (55 cm)
Note dark terminal tail band.

Bald Eagle
Haliaeetus leucocephalus
To 40 in. (1 m)

Osprey
Pandion haliaetus
To 2 ft. (60 cm)

American Kestrel
Falco sparverius
To 12 in. (30 cm)

Great Horned Owl
Bubo virginianus
To 25 in. (63 cm)
Call is a resonant –
hoo-HOO-hoooo.

Great Gray Owl
Strix nebulosa
To 33 in. (83 cm)
Large gray owl has a black and white "bow tie."

Western Meadowlark
Sturnella neglecta
To 9 in. (23 cm)

Canada Jay
Perisoreus canadensis
To 14 in. (35 cm)

Western Tanager
Piranga ludoviciana
To 7 in. (18 cm)

Clark's Nutcracker
Nucifraga columbiana
To 13 in. (33 cm)

BIRDS

Greater Sage-Grouse
Centrocercus urophasianus
To 30 in. (75 cm)

Ruffed Grouse
Bonasa umbellus
To 19 in. (48 cm)
Note black tail band.

Broad-tailed Hummingbird
Selasphorus platycercus
To 4.5 in. (11 cm)

Calliope Hummingbird
Selasphorus calliope
To 3.5 in. (9 cm)

Common Raven
Corvus corax
To 27 in. (68 cm)

Black-billed Magpie
Pica hudsonia
To 22 in. (55 cm)

Mountain Bluebird
Sialia currucoides
To 7 in. (18 cm)

Mountain Chickadee
Poecile gambeli
To 6 in. (15 cm)
Note white "eyebrow."

Yellow-headed Blackbird
Xanthocephalus xanthocephalus
To 11 in. (28 cm)

Red-winged Blackbird
Agelaius phoeniceus
To 9 in. (23 cm)

Brown-headed Cowbird
Molothrus ater
To 7 in. (18 cm)

American Robin
Turdus migratorius
To 11 in. (28 cm)

Yellow Warbler
Setophaga petechia
To 5 in. (13 cm)

Gray-crowned Rosy-Finch
Leucosticte tephrocotis
To 6 in. (15 cm)

REPTILES & AMPHIBIANS

Columbia Spotted Frog
Rana pretiosa
To 4 in. (10 cm)
Call is a series of short croaks.

Boreal Chorus Frog
Pseudacris triseriata maculata
To 1.5 in. (4 cm)

Boreal Toad
Anaxyrus boreas
To 4 in. (10 cm)
Males have a soft, clucking call.

Northern Sagebrush Lizard
Sceloporus graciosus graciosus
To 6 in. (15 cm)

Blotched Tiger Salamander
Ambystoma melanostictum
To 13 in. (33 cm)

Wandering Garter Snake
Thamnophis elegans vagrans
To 40 in. (1 m)

Valley Garter Snake
Thamnophis sirtalis fitchi
To 4 ft. (1.2 m)

MAMMALS

Little Brown Bat
Myotis lucifugus
To 3.5 in. (9 cm)

Red Squirrel
Tamiasciurus hudsonicus
To 14 in. (35 cm)

Deer Mouse
Peromyscus maniculatus
To 8 in. (20 cm)
Distinguished by its white undersides and hairy tail.

Least Chipmunk
Neotamias minimus
To 9 in. (23 cm)
Note white stripes on side and face.

Uinta Ground Squirrel
Spermophilus armatus
To 12 in. (30 cm)

Meadow Vole
Microtus pennsylvanicus
To 7 in. (18 cm)
Small mouse-like creature has long fur and a short tail.

American Pika
Ochotona princeps
To 9 in. (23 cm)
Inhabits rock piles.

MAMMALS

American Badger
Taxidea taxus To 35 in. (88 cm)

Yellow-bellied Marmot
Marmota flaviventris To 28 in. (70 cm)

Wolverine
Gulo gulo To 44 in. (1.1 m)

American Beaver
Castor canadensis To 4 ft. (1.2 m)

River Otter
Lontra canadensis
To 52 in. (1.3 m)

Muskrat
Ondatra zibethicus To 2 ft. (60 cm)
Aquatic rodent has a naked tail that is flattened on its sides.

Striped Skunk
Mephitis mephitis
To 32 in. (80 cm)

Marten
Martes americana
To 26 in. (65 cm)

Coyote
Canis latrans To 52 in. (1.3 m)

Porcupine
Erethizon dorsatum
To 3 ft. (90 cm)

Red Fox
Vulpes vulpes To 40 in. (1 m)

Gray Wolf
Canis lupus To 6.5 ft. (2 m)

Lynx
Lynx lynx To 42 in. (1.06 m)

Bobcat
Lynx rufus
To 4 ft. (1.2 m)

MAMMALS

Mountain Lion
Puma concolor To 9 ft. (2.7 m)

Grizzly Bear
Ursus arctos horribilis
To 8 ft. 2.4 m)

American Bison
Bos bison To 12 ft. (3.6 m)

Black Bear
Ursus americanus
To 6 ft. (1.8 m)

Mountain Goat
Oreamnos americanus
To 6 ft. (1.8 m)

Mule Deer
Odocoileus hemionus
To 7.5 ft. (2.3 m)

Bighorn Sheep
Ovis canadensis To 6 ft. (1.8 m)

Pronghorn
Antilocapra americana
To 5 ft. (1.5 m)

Elk
Cervus canadensis To 10 ft. (3 m)

Moose
Alces alces To 10 ft. (3 m)